Meat Rack Boy

By Michael Tarraga

DEDICATION

This book is dedicated to my twin brother and my sister. To the two I never knew.

The photo on the front cover is of my twin brother. It's the only photo I have of any of my family, including that of myself. It was given to me by Lambeth council.

INTRODUCTION

This is a short, but true story of my life — Michael Peter Tarraga. I've given my story the title *Meat Rack Boy* because that is what I was: on sale and a piece of meat. Discarded as a baby with my twin brother, whose photo is on the front cover of this book, and my two year-old sister. We were the children of a prostitute left at the hospital in which we were born, and not even taken home. Then in the 'care' of the authorities throughout my childhood and sold for sex like a piece of meat. Ripe for the plucking, a chicken. That's what they called boys like me — a 'chicken'.

A lot of people — many of whom are now very good friends of mine — think they know all there is to know about me, but some of you who read this are in for quite a surprise. Throughout my life I've learned to keep my guard up, and there's only so much that I actually allow people to see of the real Mike Tarraga, *The DJ*, the guy who clowns around while playing music, and has two skeletons for buddies. The rest of what's happened in my life has been kept under wraps from most people, except those I consider very close friends. It is shocking, and it may upset or disgust you.

There are a number of reasons for me not telling people about certain aspects of my life until now. One is, I've always doubted whether I'd be believed, and you will understand what I mean as you read on. But I give you my word: what you are about to read is the absolute truth.

Another reason is because I feel ashamed of some of the things I've done in my life. My story will shock the arses off some, but this is me — the real Mike Tarraga. I am telling my story now, because as a lot of my friends know, time is not on my side and I want to get it all off my chest now — while I sanely can.

It's not all doom and gloom, though. Those who know me well enough will not be surprised at some of the antics I've got up to. So I hope as you read my story it will bring a smile to your face. If this short memoir is well received I may decide to write a full autobiography, then maybe they'll even make a film of my life. I can just see it now—Johnny Depp as the young me and Keith Richards as the older me — I want there to be humour in this…How am I doing so far?

One guy I spoke to recently described my act as that of a 'clown'. I laughed and told him I'd always thought I was a DJ. But he'd arrived at his impression of me because of my Facebook posts — bloody Facebook!

Lastly, I make no apologies for the use of vocabulary. As anybody who knows me knows I don't do 'PC'. What you see is what you get with me… like it or lump it.

1 CHAPTER ONE
WHY NOW?

This isn't the first time I've written my life story. I wrote it many years ago, 480 pages in total, all handwritten, for a court appearance. I wrote it for the judge and, if I'm honest, I thought it might explain who I am and why I behaved this way, and he'd let me off. But do you know what happened when he read it? He called it 'this tragic document. Then sent me away for three years.

I didn't give up, however. I then took it to a national newspaper, *The Sun*, to be precise. And it was the only newspaper I approached. I met a reporter who is now a chief correspondent there. Well ,we sat on a bench in Canary Wharf, me holding my 480 handwritten pages in my hand, hoping he'd listen and finally give me a platform on which to be heard. But do you know what he said? I remember it clearly. 'Do you really expect people to believe this?' And I thought, 'Well, that's it.' It was the end for me.

He'd looked into my background and could see I had a

criminal record, and said that was that, pointless even telling my story.

And nobody did listen and nobody wanted to listen.

So what options were open to me then? Well, I spent a lot of my own money getting the book published, using a local company where I live here in Fleetwood to print it for me. It cost thousands of pounds. I gave the book away, just asking for a donation to a local charity called Sam's Place. It cost me £4000 to print the book and we made £600–700 for charity.

So here we go again, but this time my book is self-published on Amazon. So why now? Well I'm 70 this year and I am dying. It was becoming more and more important to me to tell my story, because the past was beginning to get a grip again. And I was terrified that it would blow me and my partner Georgie apart. I was getting obsessed with it, and I really felt it take over.

In the last month, thanks to social media, people are finally listening. The options are there to bypass the mainstream publications and platforms, like *The Sun*.

Just a month ago, by chance, I saw one of Jon Wedger's videos on Facebook. Jon is a former Scotland Yard detective campaigning to uncover an establishment cover-up of child abuse. I listened to what he had to say. At first, I honestly thought, 'Is this just another half-wit jumping on the band wagon?' But I listened to what he had to say, and I was impressed, really impressed, and gave him a call.

I spoke to him and he listened. Now, I'll be honest with you here, I don't have a love of the law; I didn't know if I could trust him. But I have a pal who's a copper and he kept going on saying I had to tell the story, as did his wife, also a copper. What I liked about Jon Wedger was that he was on the vice in London so he could talk the talk and walk the walk. I was not talking to a virgin in the life of a sexually abused person, you could say. He knew his stuff.

Now I can see over 30,000 people have viewed the video, and it's reached 46,000; I wasn't expecting that. I'm happy about that, but I'm also scared.

I've created a strong identity where I live — intelligent, charismatic, friendly, approachable. No one knew about my past, but it was eating away at me.

I'll be honest: I was worried that people who had come to respect and accept me for me would look at me differently after I'd told this story. I've had so many people saying 'You are brave, this is a great thing you are doing'. I disagree; it isn't. I am not brave, I am not a real good chap for bringing this out. I am just a bloke coming to the end of his life, and if this is the only way to find peace, then that is what I have to do. So, after my story is out, if people want to cross the road and avoid me, then so what?

I was getting in a dark place, and I needed this story to get out. If there was a dark hole, I'd find myself in it. I didn't want to talk to my Georgie and I didn't want to interact. But by writing it, it gets it out.

This might sound strange, but when I looked at it, I felt

proud, really proud. But I also felt embarrassed, because here I was, a bloke nearly 70 years old bearing his heart and soul — and to some extent his arse — to a world I didn't know. This was a whole new ball game.

For me personally, I have no hopes of this book achieving anything for me. But I hope that it will act as a sign to people for people who read it, that, yes. this sort of thing *did* go on, and I am sure still *does*.

All of the proceeds from this book will go to help other people tell their story like I have. We don't want the money, me and Georgie have everything we want here. We have a wonderful flat, it's our home, we rent it and we're happy here. We can't go anywhere, as I am ill; we don't even want to. We are too old and tired now. Do you know what I want to do? I want to try and alleviate this trade, I want my money to go on helping others share their story — and for the trade in children sold for sex to finally end.

Do I still think children are suffering in the same way I

did? Perhaps not at the same scale, as the homes don't exist anymore. But I am sure it goes on, it will never stop: Jon Wedger and many others have confirmed that it still goes on. If you've not got a family to back you up and you're in care, then you are ripe for plucking. We need to look after these children, children like me — who had no-one.

And, finally, another very important reason I wrote this book: to say sorry to those I've let down. It wasn't just me that suffered. I have a son who's in prison for killing someone (he was a drug addict and knifed someone for just £40) because I failed him. I failed him and many others. I kept running and I wrecked lives.

I wasn't there for him. In mind or body I walked away from his mother and from many others.

I am nearly 70 and, yes, it took a long time to get it out, but the more people who hear these things, the more chances they'll be halted. I don't want anyone who went through a third of what I went through to not be believed. I want people to listen.

Please just make your own mind up. It's taken until now to meet Jon Wedger, to use social media — to finally find the strength to tell the story, because nobody believed me. No-one listened. I felt it was a case of 'as long as it's not affecting me, I'm not worried'. But unless stories like mine get out to the mainstream public, this will carry on, big-style. I don't want anyone coming to me and saying 'You made this up, it's a load of old bollocks, to make a few quid out of it'. I don't want a bean, no expenses, nothing. I want the story told and for people then to make up their own minds.

I'll be completely frank with you. This story, my story, horrifies me. Living through it again and bringing it back is sickening. It is absolutely rotten. When I plucked up the courage to watch the interview I did with Jon, I just cried.

I just thought, 'Bloody hell. What have I done?' I don't want any money and I don't want to re-live it. I have done this because I want things to change.

2 CHAPTER TWO
UNWANTED

I was born on the 7th October 1949 at Bow Hospital in East London, one of twin boys. My brother was Stephen Mario Tarraga. We also had a sister —Melita Henrietta Tarraga — who was a couple of years older than us. She had been born on the 28th August 1947.

The name Tarraga is Spanish. Our father Mario Roberto Tarraga had come over from Spain as a refugee, fleeing the Spanish civil war. He was a Basque separatist. I found out he had managed to get a job in London working in the catering industry, but doing what exactly, I don't know.

Our mother was a prostitute. She'd travelled down from Scotland during the war, thinking there'd be more money to be made in London. How our mum and dad actually got together, none of us knew. But they did marry — albeit bigamously — on my father's side.

Three days after Mario and I were born, our mother brought Melita to the hospital. She told the staff she couldn't cope with a small child and now two babies, and on top of having us she was about to become homeless, so she had nowhere to take us. In other words, there was no home for us. She walked out, leaving the hospital staff shocked and, no doubt, distressed. All three of us were taken into care and sent together to a children's nursery in Chislehurst, Kent, where we were to spend the next three years. We never saw our mother or father again.

In 1952 all three of us were taken from the nursery to a foster home. I think Mario and I had just turned four. This was 2 Gravely Avenue in Borehamwood, Hertfordshire. The home was run by a married couple, Bob and Ivy Woods. There were seven children in total being fostered at the Woods' house. Apart from us three, all the other child residents had parents. But, for whatever reason, most of them were housed there temporarily.

3 CHAPTER THREE
HORROR AND PAIN

The foster home was funded by Lambeth Council and was operated as a family home. We were all told to call Bob and Ivy 'Mummy' and 'Daddy'. Bob and Ivy looked and appeared to be like any normal couple. On the face of it Bob was an average sort of chap. I remember he wore glasses and always smoked Capstan Full Strength cigarettes.

We hadn't been there very long when, for some reason, Stephen and Melita became very clingy towards one another. I was always a bit of a rebel and a loner and the Woods soon picked up on this. At first I was made to feel a bit special. I was allowed to stay up later than the others and watch TV and given sweets and other treats.

Although I didn't understand what was going on then, I realise now that, at the age of just four, I was being groomed. Bob started allowing me to watch TV with him. He would pull me close to him, and sometimes sit me on his knee. He often began tickling me, but that soon moved to tickling me down my pyjama bottoms. Naturally I laughed, because it tickled and felt funny; he was laughing too. I had no idea at that age that what was happening was wrong. He also encouraged me to tickle him in the same way, which I did. This made him laugh even more. I suppose it must have seemed like fun at the time.

But the fun didn't last, and it wasn't very long before things took a much more sinister course. One night I was being a bit grizzly; I was probably tired. Bob hadn't been in from work long. He worked as a security man at the Handley Page Aerodrome. I could always tell when he was arriving home: I heard his motorbike rev as he pulled up outside. He came in and gave me a cuddle, telling me how much I was going to be loved. His hands were all over the place, touching me and tickling me everywhere. He said this was part of being loved, and that I was his little boy.

Not long after he'd come in I was taken into the kitchen, where Ivy was waiting with a nice clean pair of pyjamas. They had run some warm water in the sink. Bob undressed me and stood me in the water and began washing me. Suddenly I felt the most horrendous pain. I tried to scream, but Ivy had her hand over my mouth. Bob had pushed his finger inside my bottom, thrusting it as far inside as he could get it. I tried to squirm and struggled, but I was in so much pain I could hardly move.

After it was over, I was crying. I sobbed for ages afterwards. I remember them telling me that they were cleaning me and that I was now their son. I was dried, dressed and given a drink and a sweetie. The pain seemed to slowly subside and I was left with a dull ache. Bob and Ivy sat me on the settee between them and we all watched TV together. I remember it was warm and I must have fallen asleep. That night was the beginning of the most horrible period of my life.

What I was subjected to after that was nothing less than full-blown rape. Following the incident in the sink, things moved on at a pace. I was soon introduced to oral sex. I had to masturbate both Bob and Ivy, and I was regularly buggered royally by Bob. Ivy seemed to get as much pleasure from seeing Bob do this as he did from doing it. In some ways Ivy was the main one who instigated things, especially when it came to the beatings.

There were many times when I was bleeding so badly from my bottom — due to being raped so violently — that I couldn't attend school. I was often bruised and in a lot of pain. I just had to put up with it, because if I complained Bob would bring out one of his favourite tools for punishment. One was a cricket bat that he would whack me across the backside with, but the one he liked to use the most was a large wooden spoon. Ivy used to use this spoon for lifting the sheets out of the boiler on washing days. I was often bruised as much from the beatings as I was from the sex.

I found out many years later — after asking why no-one had questioned my absence from school — that it was easy for them to get away with keeping me off. They simply told the school that I'd been moved to another home, and then when I was fit enough to go back, they said I hadn't settled in the new place or that the new home couldn't handle me and I'd come back to them. It was all lies, but Bob and Ivy were a masterclass at lying where I was concerned.

I was constantly told not to talk to anyone at all about the things that happened at home or I would be soundly beaten. I was also told that no-one would believe me anyway. They convinced me that everyone thought I was a liar and a troublemaker. And, in those days, nobody did believe anything a kid said, so what was the point? It's true I was a moody kid with a huge chip on my shoulder, but is it any wonder with what I had to go through? I had no means of escape, nor could I risk talking to anyone about my predicament.

One day, when I was six the abuse took another turn when I was called to the office. Melita was brought in and we were both told to strip naked. We were told to kiss each other and touch each other's privates. Then Bob and Ivy told us to lie down and made us perform oral sex on each other. All the time this was happening, Bob was filming it with his cine camera.

I was six when I was introduced to Paddy or 'Grandad', as I was to call him. Grandad was about 60 and had a horrible, strange smell about him. It was a mixture of alcohol, tobacco and body odour. He was always unshaven and never had much to say, but I was told that was because he was a sick man. Bob said because he was so sick, he couldn't sleep on his own, so I was told I should share his bed with him and never to say 'No' to whatever he wanted, because he was so ill. They had made a bed up for him in the office.

Believe me, sleep didn't come into it. What that dirty old bastard didn't know about abuse hadn't been invented. He was an expert at all aspects of sexual deviation. Bob had told me I was Grandad's special little chicken. I learnt sometime later that 'chicken' was the term these perverts had for us children, as we were passed around for their evil pleasure. I often heard Bob speak to someone on the 'phone saying 'I have a chicken for you.' At the time I had no idea he was referring to me.

I had been with the Woods for about a couple of years. I know Melita and Mario were still with us at this time. Ivy called me to the office and I was told that I alone was to be taken on a special outing to see 'Aunty Elsie'. I was going to see her for the first time and that I would be going on a diesel train. I'd only ever seen the old steam locomotives before, the ones that belted out lots of smoke. These diesel trains were new; they were so quiet — and no smoke. It was a real treat. Can you imagine how exciting this was for a young lad of about six to be taken on a special journey like this? I had never been back into London since the day we left Chislehurst Nursery and we were all sent to the Woods home.

I was told this was a treat for being 'a good boy'. It was a rare act of kindness (or so I thought). I was more used to getting a good beating with the bat or the spoon. Little did I know what a different story it would be on the journey home some days later.

Singled out as the only child from the home, I felt very

special to be going to Aunty Elsie's. We weren't on the diesel train long before we had to change and catch another train to Tilbury, where Aunty Elsie lived, but it was an amazing experience. It was a large house, and I can recall there were long velvet curtains. When we arrived, there were three or four men in the living room. They were drinking and smoking and chatting away; it was very smoky.

Bob told me to sit down next to one of the men. The man put his arm around me, and I can remember his words to this day…

"This one's very clean," he said, with a smile.

I looked up at him and told him that I'd had a cold bath that morning, like I did every day. And that was true: we were all made to endure a freezing cold bath every morning, head down under the water, whatever the weather, winter or summer. I remember Ivy saying to him that I was 'fresh'. I was then led to another room, where this man joined us. All there was in the room was a bed and one chair. I was lifted onto the bed and it wasn't long before I was being subjected to a horrific sexual assault. The pain was excruciating. After he had finished, more men came in and the same thing went on and on.

It was like a conveyor belt of men. When they had finished, they would each give me a half-crown, which was a lot of money to a child in those days. Of course I wasn't allowed to keep the money. Ivy used to take it off me and tell me she'd look after it for me and keep it safe, but I never saw any of the money again. Bob had taken me there to be used. As I grew older and the abuse continued, I began to realise Bob was getting paid by these men for the pleasure of using me. I was nothing more than a male prostitute or a rent boy — but one that never got paid for the service.

I was at Aunty Elsie's for a few days and cried most of the time. Then one day Ivy told me we were going back to Borehamwood. When I got back to the home I saw Melita and Mario, but I didn't want to talk to them. I couldn't understand why this was happening to me and not them. I couldn't say anything to them. They had no idea that I was hurting and bleeding. I couldn't even cuddle them. I was in a world of my own. I actually hated them. Why was I being hurt and they weren't?

But Bob and Ivy were in trouble for taking me on this excursion to Aunty Elsie's. It appears that the welfare people had made a surprise visit and the relief house mother had told them where we'd gone. It was against the rules for them to take any of us kids away on any kind of holiday without first getting permission from the welfare, and they hadn't done that. I was too young to understand any of that kind of stuff, and I was never asked any questions at the time. It was only some years later that I heard of it.

Not long after the incident with Melita and me in the office, I came home from school to find Mario and Melita gone. They had been taken to live at the All Saints Convent in Colney, London. There were two of these homes: St Raphael's and St Gabriel's. They were run by nuns. One was for boys and the other for girls, but their paths never crossed again, because the two homes were never allowed to mix. I asked why I hadn't gone. Bob had told them that I was a very disruptive child, and for that reason they didn't want me. But the real reason was Bob and Ivy woods had other plans for me. I cried for hours after. I felt so unwanted and alone. From that day on, my sexual abuse not only continued; it got much, much worse.

I regularly became a commodity for Bob and Ivy's friends to enjoy at will. I was regularly bought and sold. I was being passed around all over. One day — I think I was probably about seven years old — I was taken to an RAF camp in London. I had been there before to a Christmas Party that they laid on for the poor kids from the London area. This particular time I was lifted on to Father Christmas's knee and again I was touched; not even Santa could be kind. I was led in to a very nice room with big candle sticks and lovely paintings of old aircraft all over the walls. The carpets were plush, with deep red pile that you sank into as you walked across the room.

This was just another instance of where and when pain was inflicted on me. I was learning by now that pain was best avoided if you did as you were told (I don't do pain), so it was time to grit my teeth and close my eyes and pray that it would all soon be over with.

These men — considered pillars of the community ('decent folk'!) — were far from decent. I was raped by men from all walks of life, and people you'd least expect it from.

Around 1956/57 the LCC (London County Council) decided that all children in care should be treated, and we were taken to the circus or the ice show. In reality, these shows were nothing more than the dress rehearsals, but at least it was a day out. We were also to be taken on holiday for two weeks during the summer breaks. Sometimes it would be to a boarding house in Scarborough or Skegness; at other times it would be to a caravan or camping in a tent. I hated the tent! I always knew it would mean sharing a sleeping bag with someone.

That could be whoever offered Bob the most money, and

of course there was no getting away once you were in the tent. And if I cried out, I knew I'd be in for a beating. There was nothing those perverts wouldn't do. Every kind of child abuse took place, always accompanied by the threat of violence. I was told before being handed over to whomever that if I knew what was good for me, I had better keep my mouth shut.

I usually didn't last the two weeks. I was always sent back home after the first week for being disruptive. And it's true, I could be a right pain. I had a chip on my shoulder the size of the Isle of Man, and if anybody upset me, boy, did I let them know it. I thought nothing of damaging equipment or stealing things. It always resulted in me getting a good hiding, but there were times when I was past caring.

4 CHAPTER FOUR
TRY TELLING SOMEONE

It wasn't long returning from one of these trips, where I' d again been violently abused, that I decided to take drastic action. I had gone to school on that particular day and had lost my free dinner chitty. This was a piece of paper that allowed me a free school meal. These chits were given to all kids in care. I had to show it to the teacher and get it stamped to receive my dinner, but on this particular day I'd lost mine and that meant I had to go without my dinner.

It was bad enough having to stand there in a queue waiting for the better-off kids to get their meals first, and then for us to go up and be given whatever dregs were left. After all, I had been doing this for ages, so it wasn't as if the teachers didn't know I was a care home child. I couldn't get my head round why I couldn't have my meal. I argued and argued my case, but when I was still refused, I lost it.

That was a bad move. The Woods were informed of my bad behaviour and when I got home I was given a real good hiding by Ivy. After the beating, I was made to stand in the hallway facing the wall. I did, then when Bob came home from work, Ivy told him what had gone on at school. As I stood there I overheard Ivy tell Bob he should go and fetch the spoon. I knew I was in for an even bigger beating than Ivy had already given me.

I was dressed in just my vest and underpants, with nothing on my feet. I decided enough was enough and I made for the door. I opened it and ran as fast as I could. I think it was just before Christmas. The weather was freezing. It was sleeting and there was a thin layer of snow on the ground, but I didn't care. I just ran for my life. I don't know how far I ran, but I found myself in the village of Radlett. I looked behind me. There was no sign of Bob following me. As I slowed down, a milkman doing his rounds spotted me. He asked me what I was doing out in the freezing cold dressed like that. He was a kindly sort who could see I was frozen and in distress. He wrapped me in his coat, then drove me in his van to the police station. All the way there he was reassuring me that everything was fine, and I'd be alright now.

The policeman behind the desk asked who I was and why I had run away from home. I told him I was hurting and that I hated the Woods and wasn't going back there. I said I wanted to run away to sea. I was wrapped in a blanket and given a hot drink. Questions were asked, such as how old I was and where was home. It wasn't long before Bob Woods came through the door, all smiles and apologising to the officer, saying I was a real problem child — a liar and a troublemaker. Unfortunately for me, the officer took Bob's word for it and believed every lie he told him.

That was my first experience of trying to run away. From that day on, I realised it was no good trying to talk to the police, because they wouldn't believe a child's story over that of an adult. Children had no say in an adult's world; they were just a commodity. I suspect the main reason for that was, as an adult with the gift of the gab, like Bob Woods, he was always going to score more points than a mouthy seven-year old.

I didn't have a childhood like normal kids. I was just one of many orphaned waifs lost in a so-called civilised world, but where none of those looking after us were civilised. No-one truly loved me, and no-one cared a jot how my life was. I was nothing more than a piece of meat (a chicken) to be passed around by some of the most perverted people, who just wanted me for their own sexual gratification. None of them minded if I was hurting; to them it was just fun.

From the age of four I had known nothing but pain. Raped and abused in every conceivable manner. I was living a life that came very close to destroying me.

During the years I was with the Woods, the welfare officer made numerous visits, but I was never allowed to speak to them directly, apart from once. The conversation didn't last long, however. I was continually made out to be a liar throughout, and of course the welfare officer again took the side of the Woods, just as the police had. They went away with the opinion that I was difficult, with an aggressive nature.

Indeed, it was their opinion that I was in need of discipline. I think it was at that meeting that I first heard the saying 'Spare the rod and spoil the child'. Believe me, the rod wasn't spared and I was far from spoilt.

It was true I was a right pain and wasn't to be trusted. I had got to the point where I didn't trust anybody I met, such was the level of abuse I'd been subjected to. And the only way I could hurt them was through their pocket, so I stole from them — money or property — I didn't care. I just wanted them to suffer the way I had. But I knew I couldn't hurt those people physically, so I resorted to other methods. Believe me, you wouldn't have trusted me in your house. I would have either pinched something or deliberately smashed it. I just didn't care. It was my revenge.

5 CHAPTER FIVE
LEAVING THE WOODS AT LAST

One day, I was called to the office. Bob and Ivy were there with some people from the welfare office. I was told that the Woods had expressed a wish to adopt me as their son. At first I had no idea what was meant by 'adopt', but when it was explained to me fully I think the look on my face must have spoken volumes for how I felt about it.

As things turned out, they were refused. This meeting was where it was also mentioned that the Woods had broken the terms of their fostering agreement by taking me away on holidays without notifying or getting permission from the welfare people; this was strictly against the rules.

It was decided that I would remain in the care of the Woods for the time being, but only as a foster child. I had hoped they would have taken me somewhere else there and then, but it wasn't to be. And so I knew the abuse would go on. I didn't say anything. What was the point? I doubted anyone would believe anything I said, and it would only have meant another thrashing after the welfare people had left, so I kept my mouth shut.

It was now 1959 and I was ten. I had been with the Woods for six years and had been brutally abused throughout every one of those years, both by the Woods and by anyone else whom Bob deemed fit enough to rent me out to.

I had been raped by people who were high up in the law, the church and the police, and nobody cared. Most nights it would be Bob Woods who would come to my room to satisfy his sick pleasure. And, although it may sound strange to hear this, in some ways I felt let down when he didn't turn up. It was almost like I was looking forward to it. Of course I wasn't; I hated Bob Woods for the way he'd treated me. But, as the years had come and gone, I kind of got to know when he would be coming to my room, and if he didn't turn up, I sort of felt rejected. I would lie there on tenterhooks waiting for it to happen and it would take me ages to fall asleep.

One year after that meeting with the welfare people about the Woods' adoption plans, I got called to the office again. This time I was told I was being moved. I was taken from there to the convent, where my sister and brother had been taken some years earlier. But I hardly ever saw them, and even then only from a distance. There were two separate houses for the children at the All Saints convent in London. St Gabriel's was where the girls went and St Raphael's was for the boys. But the only time I saw my siblings was on Sundays in church, and we were kept apart the whole time.

All Saints was run by nuns. These wonderful ladies were nothing but love, but it did nothing for me. I just couldn't handle being hugged. Love to me had always come with a price-tag, and that price inevitably meant pain of one sort or another.

I know those feelings — or lack of feelings — stemmed from the life of abuse, which is all I'd known from the age of four. I was still being a pain, and when the nuns tried to tell me off, I'd just laugh at them. I remember Sister Helen once caned me with six of the best — then broke down in tears. She hugged me, this huge nun dressed in the black and white habit, like a massive penguin, and as she did she said, "You know Peter, God loves you. But right now I don't like you very much." She always called me Peter.

I was constantly stealing or causing some kind of mayhem. My behaviour was so bad at times that the nuns didn't know what to do with me. They'd call the headmaster of the local school to come into St Raphael's to discipline me, but it didn't do much good. There were many times when me and a friend of mine called Clifford Beavis would just run away and go to his aunt's. We'd have 2/6 which was half a crown (about 12 pence in today's money), jump on the green line bus to Battersea and go round to his aunt's house, but were never there long before we'd get caught and taken back.

The nuns decided I was to have a psychiatrist take a look at me. I was taken to Harley Street to be assessed by this shrink, who spoke to me for quite some time. He eventually came to the conclusion that I was unhinged — 'maladjusted' was the official term he used. After that the nuns wanted me away as soon as possible. I suspect they thought I might be bad for the other children.

Those wonderful nuns had done their best to show me love, but I just threw it back in their faces. I rejected them time and again. Obviously there was only so much they were prepared to put up with, so I was eventually moved on. I don't blame them one bit, but I'd never experienced real love before and didn't know how to cope with it. It was only some years later that I began to understand and appreciate the massive efforts they'd made to gain my trust.

6 CHAPTER SIX
A TEENAGER

I had been at All Saints Convent for around ten months before I was moved to another home called Liskeard Lodge in Blackheath. The authorities had wanted me to go to Heathermount in Sunningdale. This was a school that specialised in looking after kids with my problem, but it was full and there was a long waiting list, so I was sent to Liskeard, which was a reception home.

I was only there for about five or six months, after which I was shipped off to yet another home — well, two to be precise — because I was moved back and forth between two homes: The Hollies and Shirley Oaks. I spent the next two years of my life flitting about.

During these two years my behaviour got much worse and the homes were finding it more and more difficult to handle me. At thirteen, I was eventually sent to an approved school, which was nothing less than a prison for naughty boys. This was Chafford School for boys in Harwich, Essex.

I was worse off here than at any of the other schools. The abuse started again. The difference here was, it wasn't only the staff that abused you. They even encouraged the older boys to do it, too.

I was at Chafford for two years, until one day I couldn't take any more and I ran away. I decided I'd be better off in prison. I saw a policeman coming towards me as I stood looking at a shop window. I picked up a large stone and, as he came closer, I smashed the window. He asked me what I was planning to do next. I told him I was going to commit burglary, and was promptly arrested.

I was taken before South-Western Young Offender's court, who listened to my excuses and then asked for reports on me. He gave me a long lecture about right and wrong and then asked what sort of a life I wanted for myself. I told him I wanted to go to an approved school. I'd heard of one that was a nautical college. I was then sent to Stamford House for four months while reports were gathered about me. The nightwatchman at

Stamford turned out to be a paedophile who was on the run from prison, but Stamford House didn't know this. The guy was pure evil. He would come round to the dormitories every single night and the obvious would happen — again under the threat of violence if I were to tell anyone.

In the summer they sent me to Dymchurch in St Mary's Bay Kent for six weeks, a holiday camp. Even here I wasn't safe. The master was just as bad. He asked me to go with him into the sand dunes on the pretext of making plaster casts of badgers' and foxes' paw-prints, and like a bloody idiot I went along with it. But the only prints he wanted to make were on my arse.

After four months, I was sent back to South-western Young Offenders court, where instructions were given that I should go to the nautical school. This was a dream come true for me. Once there and settled in, I had many long talks with the old Padre who we used to call 'Chaps' and John Wort and John Campbell. They gave me the confidence to grow up, and to accept that the behaviour from both sides — both from me and from the perpetrators — was not the right way to go.

I remember the ship's captain, John Campbell, referring to deviant sexual behaviour as 'quaring'. He meant 'queering', but it was the way he spoke. He would stand on the quarterdeck and address us all. I had just arrived. He stood up there and announced

"There will be no damned quaring on my ship, do you all understand?"

The first time I had to go before him, he asked me...

"Do you smoke?"

"Yes sir," I replied.

"Filthy habit – here's ten cigarettes." He held them out towards me and I looked at him.

'What do you want?' I asked him quietly. He could tell I was wary of his offer.

"All I want young man, is for you to make something of your life, that's all."

I think that was probably the first time since being with

the nuns that I had met someone, especially a man, who wasn't after my arse.

The nautical college was run under the blue ensign of the Royal Navy. 'Chuffs' (John Campbell) would bang his fist to get his message across. We used to call him Chuffs because he had great chuffs and was always pulling on them. It was here that my life changed.

During the summer, me and some of the other lads from the college were sent on a kind of manoeuvres exercise to Devon. One night after we'd been into town, we were being driven back to camp in an old Morris van. John Wort was driving and I was messing about, hanging out of the side door of the van on the driver's side, when we saw a blue light coming up behind us. It was the police, and they were flashing for us to stop. I thought they'd seen me larking about and wanted a word.

John Wort got out and went to speak to the policeman. After a couple of minutes, the police left and John came back. He took me to one side. I thought I was in for a rollicking for fooling about, but he said

"You have a sister, don't you?"

"Yes, but I don't know her," I told him.

"Well, she's dead."

And that was it.

He then told me what had happened, She'd been murdered by her husband in Brighton. Melita was two years older than me. He said, if I wanted, they'd put me on a train back to the college, but he told me he thought that would be the wrong thing to do. I said 'No', I wanted to carry on. Strangely, I felt nothing inside. There was no emotion, no tears, just a sort of emptiness. We carried on, and I got on with what was asked of me.

I found out some years later that Melita had got a special licence to get married, and hadn't quite been married a year before she was killed. I had decided in a moment of drunkenness to find out about her, and I did. I went to Brighton, found out where she had lived in Lavender St. I found out she hadn't had any children. I also learned that the guy who killed her, her husband, had serious mental health problems.

But there was nothing I could do. I hadn't really known her. I hadn't seen her since I was a child, and that was that. It was a part of my life that was gone.

7 CHAPTER SEVEN
UNCLE TEDDY

Before I move on with my story, let me take a step back. To when I was 13.

If I'm honest, this particular incident didn't really stand out. It was just one of many episodes of abuse, when I was sold for sex. I would have blocked it out, had it not been for the fact that the man who sexually abused me went on to become the British Prime Minister from 1970 until 1974.

I am on my way out.

I have chronic COPD (chronic obstructive pulmonary disease). I want my story out. I think it has to be told. I also believe that if it happens and you bottle it up, you'll wreck your life and lots of other people's. I also know what has come out about Edward Heath since his death. I think there has been a huge cover-up, akin to what happened with Jimmy Savile who raped and sexually abused hundreds of children over decades without ever being charged or investigated. Is it that hard to believe that the former Prime Minister, Edward Heath, could be like him? Well, I have no doubt about that.

So let's talk about 'Uncle Teddy', like Bob and Ivy Woods who I had to call 'Mum' and 'Dad', along with my so-called 'Grandad' who abused me. Should I really have been surprised that I had another relative — this time an uncle?

Uncle Teddy was just one of many of I'd say hundreds who abused me. I actually spent a very short time with him. So for me, this story only stands out now, for who he became.

He did not anally rape me, or make me bruise and bleed, but I cannot forget meeting him or how it was just one of the many times I was sold — by someone who was supposed to care for me.

I was 13 or 14, at Chafford School for Boys in Ramsey near Harwich. The guy who took me gave me half a crown, Max Sharman, the Deputy Headmaster of Chafford School.

Uncle Teddy and I went swimming. I was taken to the boat, which was anchored out on the river.

We were at the sailing club called Pin Mill in Suffolk. It was the school holidays and as I didn't have a home to go to, I was taken out by the Deputy Head. Interestingly, the official records said I went home. But my argument is, how could I go home when the Council were my legal guardians? I had no home to go to.

I was 13/14, so it would have been around 1962. I just spent an afternoon with him sailing and swimming, I didn't know who he was. We were just told to call him 'Uncle Teddy'.

I remember there was another boy with me, but I can't remember his name.

What you have to remember in the '50s and early '60s is that a child in care without a family was a forgotten child. They go off the record. Because nobody cared, and it didn't matter if a child disappeared. If you disappeared, there was no-one to say 'This child has disappeared'. You didn't exist.

Those in schools and care homes had an absolute right to do what they wanted with you. It was a turkey hunt and they were rubbing their hands with glee when a child like me came into their care.

If I didn't go along with what they asked, even at that age of 13/14 at Chafford, I was going to meet with violence. You can grow immune to 'playing' to a certain extent, i.e. being rubbed down and touching, and oral sex. It was easier to go along with what they wanted and get slipped half a crown, than get a bloody good beating. The pain of being beaten lasts a long time, but the pain from doing something sexual is over and done with. Bang. It's over quicker. You might not be able to sleep that night, but it was simpler.

So what did Uncle Teddy do? All he did was dry my naked body, play with me and make me do something to him. We gave each other oral sex.

I can talk about it coldly, but I tell you if I hadn't been nutted off when I was, I would have killed someone. That's how bad it was. You bottle it up for so many years. When I was gallivanting around the world, it went out of my head. Being a drug addict made it easier, too — easier to block it out. Then I decided I didn't want to do drugs anymore, so I sat in Blackpool in a homeless hostel and blew the demons right off of me. I closed the curtains, drank coffee and fought off the memories of the past. But that's a few years and a few more pages on....

8 CHAPTER EIGHT
GOING TO SEA

After attending The National Nautical College I finally got my wish and, at 16, went to sea. I met many homosexuals at sea, but do you know, not one came on to me. I know it's wrong, but I hate homosexuality. I've grown to live with it and, to some degree, accept it. I can only assume I feel the way I do about it because of how I was treated as a child.

I was now 16 and my first job was as a galley boy on the *City of Halifax*, which today you'd call a bulk carrier. On that first voyage we were taking tractors to Canada and bringing grain back. After the *City of Halifax*, I sailed on a few similar ships, but I kept thinking back to my days at nautical school.

Every Sunday they'd show us a film and the programme always included a Pathe News documentary. Anyway, I'd seen this bloody documentary that asked us 'Do you want excitement? Do you want adventure? Join Britain's modern diesel trawler fleet!' It showed pictures of a guy in a white crew neck sweater, flat hat on, sat there rolling his cigarettes and generally having the time of his life on board this wonderfully clean, modern ship. I thought, 'I'd like some of that', so I joined. What a mistake!

I joined up and set off. I went to Iceland, to the white sea. Boy, was it rough! It was out there I learned how to drink rum and how to be sick, but on the lee side, not into the wind. I also got filled in on numerous bloody occasions. But I loved every minute of it. It was hard work. I was a deck-hand on a sidewinder trawler and as a deckhand I had to chop ice. It was also my job to keep filling the mate's mug with his tea, and in those days everything we had on board was rationed. The pay wasn't brilliant, but you could earn a few bob extra chopping the ice in the box room, or separating the livers from the cod in the gutting room. Not the best of jobs, but every little helped.

I've sailed on trawlers out of Fleetwood, Grimsby, Lowestoft, and all over the place, but there were instances when a crew member didn't want to sail the following day. It was a common occurrence that the poor old cook, the second engineer or the radio operator would take it in turns to get a good thumping, because without those guys we couldn't sail. And if at two o'clock in the morning a said member of the crew had had a skin-full ... then one of them poor buggers got it and it wasn't easy to find a replacement at the last minute.

I remember one time 'tide jumping' — joining a ship after it had already sailed. I made the big mistake of doing this once out of Aberdeen. The boat was *The Port Vale*, belonging to Consolidated Fisheries. The cook had thrown his hand in at sea. I was actually in digs in Grimsby when I got the call...

'Do you want a job as a cook?' I said right away, 'Yes.' It was good money as a cook and I was a quick learner.

'Right it's *The Port Vale*, we're going to send you up to Aberdeen to join it. The cook's been took ill.'

So it was a taxi from Grimsby to Aberdeen. The company said 'We'll give you £20, a case of beer and a bottle of rum. Off you go'.

I got there at three in the morning to find the port authorities would not let *The Port Vale* come into the harbour, so the pilot's launch had to take me out to the boat. When I got to the boat I was greeted by the ship's mate, who shouted

"Who are you?"

"I'm the cook. Your cook's been taken ill."

"Oh yeah!' he replied.

Then he threw a ladder over the side for me to climb up. As I was almost at the top he asked if I'd got my case of beer and my rum. I told him I had.

"Pass them up then," he told me. So I shouted down to the guy on the pilot to pass it up to me, and I then passed it up to the mate. When he'd safely got it, I started to climb up the ladder. I'd just got hold of the ship's rail when I was met with a full fist square in the nose and the words ringing in my ear, "Right, now fuck off!"

I fell back down onto the deck of the pilot boat, and looked at the mate.

"Take me back," I said. Lesson learned!

I think I went back to Grimsby and carried on working the trawlers out of there for a while after. Truth is, I've been on so many different types of craft and sailed all over the world. I even spent time in the Falkland Islands during the conflict in 1982. I was a crew member on board the *SS Canberra* and *The Uganda* (a passenger liner) which was being used as a troop carrier and hospital ship. I loved the Falklands and would love to have settled there one day. I went back down there working on fishery patrol vessels and lived ashore at Swan Inlet. It is probably the most tranquil place on earth I have ever visited, and I have been to some lovely places as a seaman. I've said to Georgie, if I could ever afford it, I'd take her down there.

A few years before the Falklands war, I had been at sea and was sailing out of Lowestoft at the time. I came back after three months away on a cargo ship. I was met by a neighbour who asked me if I'd seen the newspapers. I told him I'd been away. He said he thought as much, and then he broke it to me that my twin brother, Mario, had been killed by a bomb while serving with the British army in Northern Ireland.

That was a shock, but again — as with Melita's death — there were no tears. I just felt a strange emptiness, and thought to myself, 'Well, that's it. I really am alone in the world now'. I think I was more affected by Mario's death than Melita's, maybe because we were twins; I really don't know. His death had occurred some weeks before and the funeral had been over and done with. I saw no point in contacting the military. As with my sister, I hadn't seen him since childhood. I put it to the back of my mind. I probably raised a glass to him that day in a bar in Lowestoft.

9 CHAPTER NINE
MEETING MUM

All those years without a real mum and dad…I wondered what had happened to them. I felt completely alone, and dreamed of what might have been if I hadn't been abandoned at the hospital.

So eventually, when I was around 30, I tracked her down. I'd been trying to find her for years. I didn't have a clue what I'd say if I met her. I discovered she'd re-married — or rather got married — and had a hardware shop on Battersea Park Road in London.

So I went in there, had a look around and saw this woman behind the counter. I thought — you know, you get a feeling, like yesterday, I felt Chelsea were going to win, well it was the same kind of feeling — 'That's my mother'.

But I didn't say anything. A couple of weeks later I went back, and she was behind the counter and she said, "Can I help you, sir?" And I said, "You couldn't thirty years ago, so I don't suppose you can now." Then I just walked out.

And I regret that, for a long time, I felt very pleased.

I think I regret being rude to her, as things might have changed.

But you can't dwell on the mistakes you've made.

I don't know what I wanted and why I went in. At the time, I think I wanted to be extremely rude and hit her for money. If I'm honest, that's what I wanted.

But, really, when it came to the nitty-gritty, I just couldn't do it. I just thought, 'Be rude and walk away'. But I regret it. It was wrong.

So the question is, what if she'd had other children, my half-brothers and -sisters? Would I like to have met them?

Not now, no. I wouldn't like to meet any other children. It would be extremely hard to meet any children she had, who had maybe had a good life with her and her husband and explain to them what she'd done to us. And that would just wreck more lives. She was a prostitute, so I think she did have an inkling of the life that awaited us in care. But I don't expect for one minute that she knew it was going to be as bad as it was.

You know, she was a prostitute, it was her profession and she had to get rid of us. Because a child would have interfered with her trade, big-style. I suppose, in her mind, she did the best she could.

10 CHAPTER TEN
FALLING OUT WITH GOD

After years of sailing around the world, my life changed. I was 32 and working on a trawler when I was taken very ill with a serious ear infection. It was so bad I had to be airlifted to hospital (the Norfolk & Norwich). It was whilst I was there that I met a young student nurse called Helen, who was 23. It wasn't long before we started seeing each other and it got very serious very quickly.

Helen was from a farming family from Ipswich. I had nothing, but Helen's family were wealthy. They were also religious ('Happy Clappers'). I wouldn't say they were Christians: there was nothing Christian about any of them. From the first day they met me, they didn't like me. I was certainly not what they wanted for their little girl.

Unfortunately for them, things were to get much worse. We hadn't been going out long when we went round to her parents' house and announced that we'd got married. Her mother fainted on the spot. I thought it was quite funny, actually, but nobody else did.

We'd plucked two witnesses off the street and gone into Ipswich's Registry Office and got married. In those days you could buy a licence for seven shillings and sixpence — about 35p in today's money.

Why didn't they like me? Well, there were a few reasons, actually. I smoked, drank and swore a lot, but what could they expect from a seaman? The fact I was a trawler man was probably another reason they didn't like me. I had been told not to smoke in their garden, because the smoke would 'taint the roses'. I suspect they had hoped Helen would end up marrying a member of the clergy. They were snobs. They refused point blank to go into a pub for a drink, but would drink in a hotel bar.

Having said all that, these people turned out to be the biggest hypocrites I'd ever met in my life. They had three other children. Two girls, who were both teachers, but I hardly ever saw them, and a son, Philip. The son was a quantity surveyor at a firm in Ipswich.

However, the marriage didn't last long. I discovered that Helen had had a baby when she was 13. Her mother, who was a senior staff nurse at Heathrow Hospital, claimed she had no idea that Helen was pregnant. She said she thought her weight was nothing more than puppy fat. The baby was born in the bathroom at her home and was immediately adopted.

I think I could have forgiven Helen for having a baby, but not after I found out that the father of the child was Helen's brother, Philip. The parents had allowed them to share a bed, and carried on doing this even after the baby was born. Just after I had learned about the child, they took me along to a place called Sizewell Hall, run by an evangelist called Victor Jack. This man was another multi-millionaire farmer who was a big man in their church. Whether they thought he might be able to calm me down and stop me from saying anything about this awful situation, I don't know.

Victor Jack took me to one side, sat me down and tried to tell me everything was fine. He said Helen's brother, Philip, had come to God and confessed his sins and that God had forgiven him, so it was all alright.

I said, "Hold on here. There's a baby, an illegitimate baby that was born out of incest and adopted from birth. The grandfather tells you that they're sleeping together, and you write it off because they go to church?!" It really pissed me off big-style. I could not accept the hypocrisy of any of this.

At the time all this was coming out, I was back and forth to sea working the trawlers to earn a living. When I was ashore I shared a room with Helen who was living in the nurse's home. What I didn't know was the brother was sometimes coming round to the nurse's home and staying with Helen while I was away. After I found out about this, she tried telling me he had only come around to fix the car, and had just stayed the night.

You can only imagine what was happening. I was totally disgusted. It brought back a lot of stuff to me. I just couldn't and wouldn't accept it. How could a family who were pillars of the community — and they *were* pillars of the community, all professional people — how could they turn a blind eye to this? I really wanted revenge against them all for this. I didn't know whether to go to the police or not. In the end, I took off. I just walked away.

I decided, in my wisdom, to do something totally different with my life. I went to France, walked into a bar and asked where I could join up with the French Foreign Legion. A little French guy said to me…

"I will tell you where to go to join them, young man, but first I suggest you have a good drink." That night I got wasted. I woke the following morning in the barracks of the FFL, with a very large legionnaire standing over me.

"Welcome. You now belong to us."

The next six months taught me many things, including how to fight and, if necessary, how to kill a man. In those days, I was violent. I had a lot of pent-up anger still inside me from all the things that had gone on in my life. The FFL taught me discipline and that almost killed me, but most of all, it taught me how to survive. And you know what? I loved every minute of it. I met some fantastic men who became more than friends. They were more like brothers and would lay down their life for you, and me for them. After six months, I left to come back to sort out my car crash of a marriage.

Helen met me as I stepped off the ship. We sat in the car and she began by saying she had something to tell me. She said she hadn't behaved very well, and that she was only telling me because she felt it was right that she should be honest. She told me that while I'd been away she had been on holiday to Sicily with her family, and that she'd slept with a waiter at the hotel they had stayed in. She tried telling me that it only happened because she had been drinking; that was her excuse. That did it for me. Her dad was there, and I knew straightaway that he knew what had gone on and I told him as much. All he said was…

"We knew she was fraternising with one of the natives."

I gave him a right old mouthful: I told him that was called 'shagging' where I came from. I got up and walked away and I never saw her again. I received a letter about a year later telling me we were divorced. Bloody good riddance!

I decided to go back to sea and after three more years of working on ships all around the world, I came home and ended up in Eastbourne. I stayed there for a few years, and managed to set up my own little business as a fish-monger working off the back of a van. I'd become mates with a guy who decided we should have a go on one of these dating sites for a laugh. He took me along to a singles night at a club in Tonbridge where — after a few scoops of the local brew — I met a lunatic of a woman, whose name I honestly can't remember.

She was mad! But like a fool, I carried on seeing her. After about a month she was going around telling everyone we were engaged and going to be married. I was living in a bedsit at the time and she was living in a flat owned by the local council. She told me she wanted to buy her council flat, but she explained that to do that she needed to be married. That was the council rules when it came to buying properties. I thought, this could be a good little business move for me to have a share in a house. Arrangements were made and off we went and got married. It was no more than a marriage of convenience.

More or less straight after we were married, I realised this wasn't for me. I packed a bag, went off and re-joined the French Foreign Legion, leaving her in the flat. All was fine for about a year until I developed a health problem. Unfortunately the FFL won't keep you if you have health issues, so I had to leave. I came home to find that I'd lost the flat, she'd divorced me, sold it and scarpered. I ended up with nothing … again!

11 CHAPTER ELEVEN
JANE

I left Eastbourne and decided to go back to Lowestoft, signed up with a fisheries company and was fishing out of there for a while. The boat I was on was *The Hatherley*. It's now a tourist attraction in Scarborough and has been for some years. I became good pals with a lad called Tim, who was on our crew. We'd come back into port on the Good Friday, and because it was Easter Bank Holiday we weren't due to sail again until the following Tuesday, so I was at a bit of a loose end. Tim and me hit the market and had a few drinks.

"Why don't you come back and stay with us in Norwich for the weekend?" he asked.

I had nothing better to do, so I thanked him and off we went. Tim and I are still friends to this day, and all his family, too. It was a really good weekend. We went out on the piss and I met Jane, who was a friend of Tim's family. We hit it off right away.

Jane was a lot younger than me — a hell of a lot younger! We started going out. She was good fun to be around. She'd had a pretty hard upbringing. There were five daughters and a son in Jane's family, with only the dad to bring them up.

We had been going out for a bit and decided to get married. This time I was going to do it properly. It was to be the wedding of all weddings — I had *no* money — but 'Where there's a will, there's a way', as the saying goes. Anyway, the big day arrived. Jane looked lovely dressed in white. We had hired a Rolls Royce, followed by a lovely reception afterwards. When the time came to pay, I simply wrote out a cheque from my William & Glyns cheque book, smiled and left. Of course I knew it would bounce. I know it was naughty, but we were naughty back then.

Not long after, the police were knocking on my door, and I was asked to help them with their enquiries. I was charged with fraud ('paying in pecuniary advantage') and had to appear in court. As the judge was about to pass sentence, he looked across and laughed saying…

"Well, I hope the wedding was good, 'cause you are going to have twelve months to reflect on it."

Down I went and served the full 12 months. I spent the entire time in solitary confinement, largely due to my refusal to be co-operative with anything and because I refused to share a cell with anyone. Jane stood by me the whole time I was inside — fair play to her. But when I came out, it didn't feel the same; the spark had gone. I gave her the big heave-ho and we split up. We did get back together again and that lasted about another year, during which time our son was born.

But I was unsettled and I knew it was time for me to move on again. I didn't say anything to Jane. I just said I was going out for a packet of fags and I never went back — well, not for five years. And when I did return, she opened the door and said sarcastically…

"Did you get your fags, then?" and shut the door in my face. That was that. She'd also had a couple more kids by then, with somebody else. We stayed married for a few years until I could afford to pay for a divorce. But we've stayed friends right up to this day.

12 CHAPTER TWELVE

Meeting my Rock – Georgie

(Bird, not Geezer)

On 7th March 2007, my seafaring days came to a sudden and painful end. I was working on an oil supply ship out of Aberdeen when I had a serious accident. None of the crew on board could speak a word of English and, as the orders were being given, there was some kind of mis-communication that ended up with me being crushed against the back of the ship. I was in a very bad way and was rushed to hospital in Aberdeen.

After I was discharged from hospital, I had no job to go to, no home and absolutely no money. It was a case of beg, steal and borrow to get by. It wasn't long before I had gone wild again. I was not in a good place. I'd got myself heavily into drugs — anything I could get my hands on. I even smoked cobwebs, 'cause I was told you could, but that's rubbish. I put 240 volts to my head because I was told it would make me high, when in fact all it did was put me flat on my back and give me one almighty fucking headache.

I wandered all over the country, living rough, and ended up in Blackpool. I'd stayed at the fisherman's mission in Fleetwood many years before when I was just a rooky deckhand on the trawlers. It was half a crown to share a room and three shillings and sixpence for a single room in those days, but I remembered how kind the people had been to me then. I made my way to Fleetwood, only to find the mission had closed some years before and was now offices.

I was desperate, hungry, and quite ill by this time. I'd been diagnosed with cancer and COPD, Chronic Obstructive Pulmonary Disease. I was also violent, because I was off my head so much. I went to the Salvation Army, where someone told me they'd take me along to the council place in South King Street. We went along and I was told there was nothing they could do. I said to them…

"Well, actually you're going to have to do something, 'cause I have cancer and COPD."

It was now wintertime, January, and it was freezing. I said to them, "If I have to spend one more night on the streets, I'll be dead". I showed them a letter that I had with me from a hospital in Torquay, where I'd had a big tumour removed from my back. I'd left Torquay purposely because of the drug situation down there.

They looked at me and said…

"Right, come back at 4 o'clock and we'll find you a bed."

I went back as told, and they put me up in a night-shelter. I'd never been in a night-shelter before in my life, and it seemed alright. I thought, 'I can handle this'. There was a lounge with Sky TV. I was given a bed in my own cubicle, and a hot meal. They even did all my washing overnight and returned it the following morning clean and ironed, and I was given breakfast.

After breakfast I was told I had to go to South King Street for 9 o'clock. I went along there and was told that somebody was coming to see me from the Astley Foundation. I had never heard of them. Apparently they had places for the homeless — hostels and flats, that kind of thing. They have homes in Blackpool, Blackburn and a few other towns. It was decided they were going to put me in Oak House, and as much as I hate to say it, I hated the place, absolutely hated it. But those people there saved my life.

I had been signed on the sick, so I had a small income, but while I was staying there I had to pay so much out of my sick money to the Astley Foundation. I think it was about £20 a week, which was quite a lot of money considering the amount I was getting, and it didn't leave me a lot. They hadn't a clue I was on drugs, not until one day they decided to do random drug tests on us all. Blackpool is rife with drugs, so it was a precautionary test. It wasn't because they suspected me or anyone else was using. However, when they tested me, the readings were sky-high: I proved positive for virtually every drug going.

After the testing, I became more and more agitated. One day I was on kitchen duties — we had a communal kitchen — and took turns to cook. I was on a dairy-free diet because of my health problems and this particular day we were making shepherd's pie for tea, with a cheese topping. I told them not to put cheese on mine, just to leave a portion in a bowl for me.

When it came to teatime, I was given a bowl of cold pilchards. I looked at it and asked her, "What is that?"

"That's your tea," she said.

I complained and told her I was entitled to a hot meal the same as everyone else. It was wintertime, after all.

"No, that's your tea." She got very stroppy about it and walked off to the kitchen. I was blazing mad. I followed her, grabbed her by the throat, pushed her against the wall, picked up a kitchen knife and said...

"Pick your windows."

"Why, what are you going to do?"

She was shaking like a leaf.

I told her I was going to put her head through one window and her body through the other. Then, suddenly, I realised what I was doing and let her go. I walked into the office and said to the staff…

"I think you'd better talk to her and sort something out."

What I did was wrong, I know that, but I just saw red. It was very wrong of me. I have never hit a woman, or threatened a woman in my life; it's not my style and I totally regret it. I apologised to her later in front of Debbie Ellis, who was the manager there. And to be fair to her, she hadn't said anything about the incident and I don't think she was going to, but when it did come out, Debbie said…

"I think you need to see a doctor."

The following morning I was in Parkwood Psychiatric hospital. I was a right mess, what with all the drugs and my other illnesses. Thankfully, they sorted me out. Shortly after I went in there, I was in the dining room talking to a guy when I spotted a young woman sat at a table who really caught my eye. I turned to this bloke and said "I'm going to have her." "Not before me you're not," he said.

The following morning I was up really early and I'd gone

out into the gardens for a fag, and there she was.

"Have you wet the bed, girl?" I asked her. She laughed, we shared a cigarette, and that was that. That woman was Georgie, and we've been together ever since. I can honestly say that I have never been happier or more settled than I have been these past nine years.

13 CHAPTER THIRTEEN

The Successful Bit

On the day I left Parkwood, I gave Georgie a mobile phone, and every day I would ring her up and sing to her. She used to put the 'phone on loudspeaker so everyone could hear, and I could hear them all laughing. When Georgie came out, we managed to find a flat in Blackpool. We had nothing at all for the first two or three days — not as much as a teaspoon.

The flat leaked like a sieve. We sat in the lounge that first night and it was raining really hard. We had eight or nine buckets all over the floor catching the drips, and we had to keep moving the sofa around the room to find a dry spot. There was no heating in there either. We were freezing! But eventually we got sorted. We were taken to see Jim Parr, who owns Farmer Parr's Animal World. As well as owning the Animal World, he was a social landlord. He offered us a flat up at the farm, which we looked at, but really didn't like; it was far too small. It reminded me of a prison cell and I'd seen enough of them to last me a while.

He told us he had another place empty in Fleetwood, but it was a big flat. I think he thought it was probably far too big for the two of us, but he asked anyway if we wanted to see it. We said 'Yes, we'd like to have a look at it'. It was four o'clock in the afternoon when we went round to see it. As soon as he opened the bottom door, I knew right away that this was where I wanted to be, and I said 'Yes we'll have it'.

We had no money for a deposit or bond or rent, or anything like that, and I hadn't a clue where I'd get the money from, but he handed us the keys and said…

"There you are, move in when you want."

On the way back to Blackpool, Georgie rang the removal men and got them to meet us at our old leaky flat. This they did, and we collected all the bits and pieces of furniture that we'd managed to get together. We packed our clothes, loaded them in the van and we were in our new place by 10 o'clock that night. We actually slept on the floor in the lounge on that first night.

And we've been here ever since — not on the floor, in the flat.

It wasn't long after moving in that I became seriously ill again. I went to the doctor, and he sent me straight along to Blackpool Victoria Hospital, where I was given an X-ray followed by a scan, which suggested I had lung cancer. They then tried four times to take biopsies but missed the target every time. I was in such bad shape by this time that they decided to operate. They ended up removing three-quarters of my lung. Even then they cocked it up, because they didn't get the pieces they needed to; they admitted that. I knew then, even if the operation had been a success, that there was never any chance of me going to sea again.

So I thought to myself, 'What am I going to do now?' I thought, 'I know, I like music I'll become a DJ', and that's exactly what I did. I was, and still am, the world's worst. Fortunately I had received some compensation for the accident I'd had in Aberdeen. I spent eight grand and bought myself a Bentley. I'd always wanted one, and this one was a steal.

I also bought some disco equipment. I was seriously awful at it, but for some strange reason I went down really well. I was determined from the start that I would only play the music that I liked and that is '60s and '70s stuff, and on top of that I don't do 'PC', so if anybody argued, I'd tell them where to go and this seemed to go down a storm with the audience. But I wasn't doing it as an act; it's just the way I am. I simply don't do political correctness.

Word seemed to get around about me. I'd been asked to do a gig at the Strawberry Gardens Beer festival. It was a five-day event and I thought I'd be lucky if I lasted the first day, but the people were up on the tables…it was rocking! They loved it. I never got paid, but I didn't care.

I then bought two skeletons. The first one was Banjo Bones Marley, who came from America, and then came Alphon's Bones Marley, the brother's son who came from the Deep South. So much fun, the people loved them.

I had it in my head that I was a show business

personality, and I felt I needed something more. It was my view that when people go to a disco in a pub or a club, they want a show. I never did karaoke: I refused to. I used to sing myself, but I am not a singer, believe me, but it was fun, and it worked. I then came up with the idea that I should dress up in way out costumes, and the whole thing just got more and more crazy. But the crazier it got, the better the public liked it. I was a victim of my own success.

I've never charged for the shows I've done. Well, maybe for just for one or two, if I was skint, but certainly never for charity do's. My theory for not charging is this: if they're paying you, you have to play what they want. He who pays the piper calls the tune. But if they *aren't* paying you, you can play what the hell you want and they can't complain. I love music and I believe that music should be shared, not bought.

I've done discos all over the Blackpool and Fleetwood area and loved every minute of it, but my health has been continually deteriorating. The cancer has spread and I've had bits chopped off here and there, but the bastard keeps reappearing. In 2016, I was beginning to find it very tiring. Carting all the heavy disco equipment around was becoming impossible for me, so I took the reluctant decision to call it a day.

By this time, though, I'd accumulated thousands of pounds worth of decks, speakers, amps and lights, not to mention CDs and records. I've kept my CDs and records. And the skeletons. But the rest has gone — most of it just given away.

As long as I'm fit enough, I will still do certain things for charitable events, and for friends, but these days it has to be at a venue that has its own gear. I love nothing more than going along and causing mayhem. I have made some really good friends along the way, but the best one of them all is my Georgie.

I don't want the people who know me to see me as someone different. It's only when we came out of the lunatic asylum, Georgie and I, that my life of lunacy kind of stopped. Georgia is now 61 and I am 70 this year.

It's all down to her. I met a fellow nutter and that's how I have been able to find the strength to write this book. I met her and we kind of bonded. We had nothing — and I mean nothing — when we came out. We were lucky and found somewhere and we've turned it into a lovely home. We have been together for 11 years and have never had an argument, as we can't be arsed to argue.

The anger of what happened to me, and the violence, and the drugs just stopped. It all just stopped when I met Georgie. I couldn't run away any more from what had happened. I had finally found comfort and peace.

We both had difficult backgrounds and we were both honest with each other. I did not want a one-night stand. I wanted someone to look after, and to look after me. I really didn't expect it to happen. I'd just gone through my life wrecking other people's.

She accepted me. She knew I was penniless and had nothing. I knew she was the same. And we thought, 'Right, if we are starting from zilch, we have no expectations of each other'. We could have both left each other at any time, but we care for each other and love each other.

Why did I trust her? I don't know. There was something in me that said, 'She is going to be alright', and she is. I honestly don't know. She is still under the shrinks and they can't fathom it out. We were told right from the off that we shouldn't be together.

The shrinks did everything they could to keep us apart. I don't know why.

I think it was because I have some knowledge of the law. They were going to throw Georgie out of the hospital and put her on a bus to London. I marched into the consultants who'd threatened to section her and asked what the diagnosis was. They didn't know.

So I said, 'How can you throw her out? This is illegal to have no roof over your head and no income. It's a criminal offence, for which you can be jailed'. I said to the consultant, 'You'll be committing a criminal act, by conspiring to make her a vagabond'. It's funny: it was only then that I got sent to the 'funny farm', the mental hospital.

Then I came off the drugs completely and I was stone cold sober, and have been ever since. I met Georgie and we have a home together and we are very proud of what we have.

I don't want money. I want my story to be told. I need my story to be told before I die. I really wanted my story to get out — to a documentary maker.

When you get to an age when you can tell it to someone who believes you, it sets you free. I did contact the police and spent hours telling them everything. But within three weeks, they told me, 'Because the perpetrators are dead, there can be no case'. But I have social media now, so I can publish my story online.

Epilogue

For a number of years now, I, along with many others who were in the care of Lambeth Council, have been fighting for justice. Hundreds, if not thousands, of children like me were abused in care — violently, physically, sexually and mentally abused, and nobody listened. I survived, but I am sure some didn't as a result of the abuse they suffered.

While it has been accepted that I was in care and that I was abused during that time, there are few records to be found of where I was and when. Even the police weren't helpful. They and their solicitors told me that everyone who may have been guilty of any wrongs are now all dead and that I should leave it alone. Sorry, I can't do that.

I want justice for me and for all the others who were hurt. And if my pursuit of that justice helps to highlight these terrible wrongdoings and prevents one more child from going through what happened to me, then I will have achieved something worthwhile. My fight is still going on today in 2017.

UPDATE January 2019 – this has been written following the 13 January 2019 Facebook Live interview with Jon Wedger, which at the time of publication has reached 50,000 people.

How do I feel about Bob and Ivy Woods? Sadness, pity. There is no anger there. It's gone. I don't have anger any more. If you hurt someone in retribution, what do you gain from it? Nothing. With this book, I'm absolutely sure you've got abusers who are reading it, and abusers who have watched the video interview I did with Jon Wedger and, no doubt, they'll be reading the comments. Even if just one of them realises the damage they're causing and knocks it on the head, I will be happy. Even if it stops just one person. That would be a result.

End-note

When I look back, I ask myself 'What was the most painful episode of abuse ever?'

Being filmed as a youngster doing things to my sister; that, for me, was the worst. But I'll be honest: one thing that I will never forget when I really hit rock-bottom was knowing that I couldn't drop any lower. Reality set in, and I was in a deep, dark place.

But something made me come back up again.

So this book is a result of hope — a hope that I can inspire everyone who reads it to finally do something about the horrific abuse of children in care who, like me, had no-one.

Well, now you've read this book, I hope they have you.

Thank you.

By MICHAEL TARRAGA